Going Places

Going Places

Poems by

William Heath

© 2023 William Heath. All rights reserved.
This material may not be reproduced in any form, published,
reprinted, recorded, performed, broadcast,
rewritten or redistributed without
the explicit permission of William Heath.
All such actions are strictly prohibited by law.

Cover design by Shay Culligan
Cover photo by Josep Caminals of the author, his wife Roser,
and her mother Antonia at Au Pied de Cochon in Paris
Author photo by Josep Caminals

ISBN: 978-1-63980-281-4

Kelsay Books
502 South 1040 East, A-119
American Fork, Utah 84003
Kelsaybooks.com

To Paul Blackburn and Phil Levine, who told me I should go to Barcelona, and to Senator Fulbright who made it possible.

With thanks for their invaluable assistance to Esperanza Hope Snyder, Holly and Frank Bergon, David Salner, Neal Learner, Marty Malone, and my beloved co-conspirator Roser Caminals-Heath.

*The man who finds his country sweet is only a raw beginner;
the man for whom each country is as his own is already strong,
but only the man for whom the whole world is as a foreign country
is perfect.*
—Hugh of St. Victor, 12th century

Acknowledgments

Apricity Magazine: "Plaça Reial"
Arlington Literary Journal: "Puerto de Santa María," "The Death of Marco Polo"
Atlanta Review: "The Dutch Masters"
Bells: "Topless Beach," "The Shining Path"
Cathexis Northwest: "Rimbaud in Abyssinia"
Change Seven: "In the Pyrenees"
Clackamas Literary Review: "On the Nile"
Concho River Review: "Last Visit to Barcelona"
The Cooke Book: An Anthology of Maryland Poets: "At the Sauna"
The Courtland Review: "Travel"
Door Is A Jar: "Islamabad," "Bolivia"
Eye to the Telescope: "In Quest of Yeti"
Evening Street Review: "How It's Done"
Exit 13: "A Night at Smarkand's Starless Hotel"
Glimpse: "Incidents on the Ivory Coast"
Illuminations: "The Wailing Wall," "Swatting Flies," "Santo Domingo"
Innisfree 31: "How to Catch an Anaconda"
In Parentheses: "Will Andrei Amalrik Survive Until 1984?," "A Brief Tour of Italy"
Leaving Seville, a chapbook: "Our Lady of Flamenco," "Three Kings in Seville," "Tear Gas," "The Uncouth Coup," "Six Bulls," "A Few Crucifixions," "Maro," "Paseos," "Leaving Seville," "Roser Plays the Field," "Roser," "The Gift"
Litbreak Magazine: "Growing Tomatoes in Nigeria," "Odysseus Returns"
MacQueen's Quinterly: "G.I. Joe in Naples, 1944," "Banksy's Prank"
Mediterranean Poetry: "Balcony of Europe," "The Little Barber at War"
Midwest Quarterly: "Yes and No"
The Orchards Poetry Journal: "Easter Island"

Plainsongs: "Saffron Walden"
Pulsebeat Poetry Journal: "Aureli's Funeral," "Barrio de Santa Cruz"
Quadrant: "Before the Revolution," "A Trip to Flanders," "Remembering the Great War"
Schuylkill Valley Journal: "Afghanistan"
Slippery Elm: "Cargo Cult"
Sunlight Press: "Queen Nefertari's Tomb"
Tipton Poetry Journal: "The Women of Tehran"
Wisconsin Review: "Taking Pictures," "The Perfect Shower"

Contents

I Leaving Seville

Our Lady of Flamenco	17
Three Kings in Seville	18
Barrio de Santa Cruz	19
Plaza Doña Elvira	20
Calle Mármoles	21
At the Sauna	22
Tear Gas	23
The Uncouth Coup	25
Six Bulls	27
A Few Crucifixions, Some Processions	29
Feria	33
Picking Olives in Andalusia	36
Maro	38
Balcony of Europe	40
Swatting Flies in Spain	41
Topless Beach	42
Puerto de Santa María	43
Paseos	44
Palma del Río	45
A Trip to Madrid	49
Jerez de los Caballeros	50
Leaving Seville	51

II Barcelona Posa't Guapa

Plaça Reial	55
Roser Plays the Field	56
Roser	57
The Gift	58
María	59
Francesca's Secret	61

The Little Barber at War	62
In the Pyrenees	64
Taking Pictures	66
The Referendum	69
Aureli's Funeral	70
Some Sayings	71
On Pets	73
Pickpockets	75
Last Visit to Barcelona	76

III Travel

Travel	79
The Perfect Shower	80
The George, or Farewell to Merry Old England	81
On Hamlet	82
Mind the Gap	83
Saffron Walden	84
Banksy's Prank	85
The Berlin Wall	86
That Summer in Paris	88
How It's Done	92
A Brief Tour of Italy	93
G.I. Joe in Naples, 1944	95
The Death of Marco Polo	97
The Dutch Masters	98
A Soldier in the Great War	99
Before the Revolution	108
Will Andrei Amalrik Survive Until 1984?	109
Odysseus Returns	112

IV Walkabout

The Wailing Wall	115
Yes and No	116
On the Nile	118
Queen Nefertari's Tomb	120
The Women of Tehran	125
Islamabad	126
Afghanistan	128
An Outpost of Allah	129
A Night at Samarkand's Starless Hotel	130
In India	131
Gandhi and the Robber	132
In Quest of Yeti	133
Japanese Watercolor	134
How to Capture an Anaconda	135
Incidents on the Ivory Coast	136
Growing Tomatoes in Nigeria	137
Rimbaud in Abyssinia	139
Santo Domingo	142
Yucatán	143
Chichén Itzá	144
Guatemala	146
The Shining Path	148
Bolivia	150
Vietnam	151
Walkabout	153
Easter Island	154
Cargo Cult	155
Fossil Time	156

I
Leaving Seville

Our Lady of Flamenco

I hear talk about flamenco—
how the woman knows when
to lift her skirt, how to let
her hands come alive in the air,
fingers spiraling and snapping,
uplifted arms swaying slowly—
a woman maybe in her forties,
full-breasted, wide-hipped,
dancing with two men half her age
and filling them with a foot-
stamping desire everyone
in the audience can feel,
while the hands smack out
an intricate rhythm—clapping
faster and louder than any
music mere hands could make,
yet did, filling the whole room
with it—until all were drawn
to their feet to be dancers, too,
fingers snapping, feet beating
on the floor an insistent lust
for life itself. All this one woman,
with swirling skirts, sure steps,
and head held as high as pride
and passion would allow, all this
one woman accomplished by
mastering the voluptuous
movements of her turning,
unfurling, *duende* dance.

Three Kings in Seville

Eve of the Three Kings, streets
packed with children in
tent-like blue or green coats.
A balloon soars above La Giralda,

a police car, blue-lights flashing,
five officers on white horses
clear a path for marching bands
and floats with girls in white.

Interspersed along the way
a float bearing a king, the black
one the popular favorite—
a simple, effective way to dispel

racism before it festers.
I am struck by how the girls
toss candy to eager children
along the route. Aloof, unsmiling,

receiving adoration as their due,
the idea of joyfully responding
past thinking. They disperse
their treats sparingly, disdaining

most outstretched hands,
each young beauty a princess
on a royal progress, satisfying
her subjects beneath her dignity.

On my own in Seville, puzzled
by the mystery of Spanish women,
I see them as a clue.

Barrio de Santa Cruz

In Spain the rain falls mainly
in the mountains and the pain
is on display in the streets.
Like any Ohio boy, the first time
a gypsy holds out her hand
I shake it. Watch your wallet,
I learn. Never look a beggar
in the eye. The mother gives
her child a cardboard sign,
soy una pobre niña, shows
how to expose one bare foot
beneath a shawl full of holes,
slaps her to make her cry.
The child is quick to sort
the tossed coins, gathering
the larger ones out of sight
then resuming the lost look
her mother taught her
works best, but today she is
shivering in the cold,
a more effective look
her skin will not forget
nor her freezing bones
when she is a woman grown,
teaching her poor daughter
how to beg in the street.

Plaza Doña Elvira

If Seville is a city of secrets—especially
the old Jewish quarter of Santz Cruz
with its winding back streets, white-
washed buildings, wrought-iron balconies
packed with flower pots, and barred windows
where once would-be Don Juans "ate iron"
courting señoritas—then Plaza Doña Elvira
is the inner sanctum.

For me it is a tranquil place at the heart of
the labyrinth, the snug secluded square has
a pink marble fountain at the center flanked
by stone benches and shaded by orange trees
whose blossoms anoint the air in the spring
while the ripe fruit has a destiny as marmalade.
I love to watch the watery arrows shoot
skyward against the silken air and collapse
onto themselves with a musical plash.

After a fourteenth-century pogrom drove out
the residents, King Enrique III gave the land
to Don Pedro López and over the centuries
it was renovated to form the present plaza
named after the Don's daughter, since she,
an object of his fickle desire, plays an integral
part in the legend of Don Juan and figures
in the famed dramas of Tirso de Molina, Zorrilla,
Molière, as well as Mozart's great opera.

No wonder Plaza Doña Elvira possesses
an esoteric charm all its own. Or so it once
seemed to me. Nowadays it is ravished
by tourists, its secret open to all comers.

Calle Mármoles

A few blocks from where I live
in Santa Cruz I pass a boarded-up
vacant lot like the ones I'd seen
in American cities—old doors form
the walls, green sludge, a sprinkling
of Coke cans in the hole left after
a structure was torn down. Only
this excavation bottoms out some
fifteen feet below street level,
while rising from the muck are three
Roman columns of Egyptian granite
at least twenty-five feet high.

The street is named for these ruins,
albeit the three columns aren't of marble,
no tourists come. They're simply
a reminder of why Seville will never
have a subway—anywhere you dig
you hit layers of previous civilizations.

I do some digging to uncover the story:
originally part of the portico of a temple
in Itálica, the nearby Roman city,
birthplace of Trajan and Hadrian,
six columns were brought to Seville
to help support a medieval building.
In the sixteenth century one was broken
and abandoned, two, topped by sculptures
of Julius Caesar and Hercules, now flank
the gateway to the Alameda, the other three
are remnants of a demolished palace.

There they stand, flat-topped heads
bereft of their proud Corinthian crowns,
feet sunk in the green sludge of near oblivion.

At the Sauna

We men sit on hot planks
at the sauna and talk
of how hard it is here
in Andalusía to find work.
Where are you from they ask
and when I tell them
they rub their sweaty
fingers together to show
how rich they think I am.
I am not a rich man
and the sweat runs down
into my eyes until I weep
and the men shift positions
as someone tosses more
water on the hot rocks
and the sweat pours down
all our bodies. There is no work
in Andalusía and the water
in the shower is always cold.
As I shiver on the cold boards
in the drying room and watch
the steam rise from my body
I think of a woman who will
never come to Andalusía
and as the men keep on talking
I know for certain that I
am not a rich man.

Tear Gas

You've seen this picture before:
English class sitting on the grass,
books open in laps, professor
and students engaged in discussion.
Now add a line of national guardsmen
in masks, spraying them with tear gas.
The scene a campus in Lexington
the May day the sixties ended, four
dead at Kent State, everyone protesting
Nixon's incursion into Cambodia.

Here's what tear gas taught me:
eyes stinging, it compels retreat
but also instills an intense
chemically induced fury to smash
what's at hand, that's why
peaceful demonstrators so attacked
might go berserk. Being gassed
and the March on Washington
are my sixties badges of honor.
Of others, less honorable, I am silent.

Seville, 1980. Like Charlie Chaplin
in *Modern Times,* walking to class I'm swept
along by a protest march going my way.
At the university troops block the street.
Our leaders order us to sit down.
Tear gas grenades soar in the air,
but it's a windy day, they veer
off target into the courtyard of
Alfonso XIII, a five-star hotel,
coddled guests scurry for cover.

That whiff of tear gas doesn't enrage me.
How could it? I'm laughing too hard.
Then the troops advance. People scream,
begin to run. I leap on top of the wall
enclosing the university, look up,
from a window my English colleagues
implore me to escape. Finally safe
in the office, only a torn shirt to prove
my adventure, nonchalantly I remark,
"Hey, man, just like the sixties."

The Uncouth Coup

23 February 1981

I should be suspicious
when I see the empty streets
and an eerie silence pervades
old Seville, but I'm not alarmed
until I see that the university—
a building that fills a city block,
where I teach my classes,
where two centuries ago real
Carmens rolled tobacco leaves on
their inner thighs to make cigars—
is completely dark.

                At my local
bar I am greeted with *"Adiós,
democracia,"* due to a coup.
Rebellious soldiers have taken
the Congress in Madrid hostage
and tanks invade the heart
of Valencia. Back in my room
the radio plays marching music
and at nine, instead of the news,
The Princess and the Pirate, a Bob
Hope comedy, is on television.
Imagine how horrifying that is.
They, whoever *they* are, now
control the national media.

What will come next? Several
anxious hours later King Juan Carlos,
in full military regalia, appears
on television, demands loyalty
from the army, and stops the coup,
which has been caught on camera.

The next day we watch a pistol-
waving Colonel Tejero's civil guards
burst in on a session of parliament
voting for prime minister. When Tejero
orders the deputies to hit the floor,
he is resisted by a few brave men
of opposing parties. A submachine gun
is fired at the ceiling, an elderly deputy
is affronted, the duped troops
drain a liquor cabinet, bail out
back windows.

                    After the surrender
Spaniards agree that the failed coup
hasn't been done properly, there *must*
be a better way to do such things.
That evening the bartender offers me
a *"Tejerito"*—holding up a bottle
whose cork is elaborately carved
into the face of a man, topped by
the tricorn cap of a civil guard,
featuring a massive mustache beneath
the droopy eyes of a bandito who
botched his big chance.

Six Bulls

1

The first bull charges fiercely
into the ring, asserting sole
possession of its territory.
The torero waves his cape,
offering a futile chance
to destroy an intruder.
Then the banderillero
dances by on tiptoe before
sticking his barbed darts,
leaving the bull to confront
a picador on a padded horse,
which the bull lifts easily
in the air by the powerful
force of its neck. The picador,
unperturbed, leans over, jabs
his long pointed pole into
the bull's upper back muscles,
spilling blood down its sides,
as the mad, baffled animal
finally faces the torero,
who lures him into turns
and counterturns to chase
an elusive cape whirling
before enraged eyes, as the man
spins past searching horns.

2

At first sight of the ferocity
of the six bulls, I sympathize
with the torero, as the cruel
ritual pursues a relentless end,
I pity the deluded bulls. They
drool, piss, bleed, roar, chase
cape after cape, lift this horse,
smash that wall, suffer gruesome
wounds, draining them of strength.
In time each bull lowers its horns,
receives for his pains a sword
thrust up to the hilt aimed for
the heart. Initially unfazed,
turning in a circle of capes,
soon each drops to its knees
in midcharge, a knife delivers
the coup to grâce. Three mules
drag the carcass out, leaving
a red trail in the dust. His slayer
in skintight white satin pants,
gold-braided jacket, a blood
smear by his crotch, a sock ripped,
a cut on his shin, struts around
the ring brandishing his trophy,
a severed ear, as the crowd rises
to its feet, chants his praises,
and I seek the nearest exit.

A Few Crucifixions, Some Processions

1

Mary, a sword through her heart,
gazes up at Christ crucified;
at his feet, plastic arms, legs, heads
of people afflicted in those parts.

Mary, one foot on a serpent
biting an apple, holds her child,
whose chubby fingers pluck
a cross as if it were a harp.

Christ stretched so far he's cracked
at the armpits, three Cupids below
scrub up in a tub beside a saint,
his raised hand blesses the soap.

One Christ is strapped to the cross
with ropes to prevent drooping,
another has scraped knees,
a line of blood down each shin.

A side altar displays in gold
all the instruments of torture:
spikes, spear, sponge, hammer,
scourge, tongs, crown of thorns.

2

By day and night during Holy Week
long lines of dark-robed Merlins in
conical caps, a six-foot candle jutting
from the hip, process in pairs through
the streets of old Seville; masked penitents
wearing a cowl walk barefoot, carry
a wooden cross. Each church has
two sumptuous floats, one depicts
Christ's last days in Jerusalem
from donkey entry to the crucifixion;
the other is devoted to Mary.
The carved figures are life-size,
most floats weigh a ton or more.

I like to watch the floats snake
down the winding street aptly named Sierpes,
the spine of the commercial district,
or from a rooftop in Barrio de Santa Cruz
where I can see them enter the Cathedral
to be blessed before their return journey.
The climax of Semana Santa comes in
the early morning hours of Good Friday,
when the popular favorites, and mine—
Jesús del Gran Poder and La Macarena—
are processing in the heart of the city.

He stands on a golden baroque float,
dressed in a vivid purple tunic, a thick
noose around his neck, both hands
on a cross depressing one shoulder,
blood on his forehead from his crown
of thorns, agony in his eyes, teeth
and tongue showing his ordeal,

even his bare feet convey suffering.
A pervasive odor of incense.
Muffled drums sound a solemn dirge.

She appears beneath a fringed canopy
supported by a dozen silver pillars,
her eyes have life-like lashes, cheeks
are rouged, tears glitter like diamonds.
A gem-encrusted satin gown, a jeweled
rosary in her hands, the silver float
is banked with flowers and candelabra.
A talented soloist in a balcony "spontaneously"
lets fly an arrow-like song of adoration.
In honor of her beauty, the crowd chants,
"Guapa . . . guapa, guapa, guapa."
Aroma of lilies and candle wax.
Her band plays an upbeat tune.

Yet Seville is not very religious.
A few women attend mass. Lift
the brocade skirt beneath the float
and see another story. The burly men
bearing the brunt of the weight,
a padded turban on head and neck,
wearing work pants and sandals,
stop at a every bar for a quick
beer and smoke. Many are Communists,
never step inside a church; they do
this back-breaking labor for pay
or out of loyalty to their barrio.
Some make the Virgin's float sway
so she shimmies and shakes.
The air smells of sweaty men.

3

After a week of festivities,
work crews spend days
sweeping up smashed bottles,
scraping wax from the streets.

Feria

The best way to learn Spanish
is an *intercambio*. My partner
is Carmen (she goes by Menchu).
One day in the gardens of the Alcázar,
whose 14th-century stone walls
border Barrio de Santa Cruz, she dances
a sevillana before a marble fountain,
sunbeams through the orange trees
make the spouting water sparkle.

She shows me how to hold my hands
above my head and attempt the city's
signature dance combining four *coplas*.
Each stanza with an intricate nine-step
choreography calls for the couple
to pass back and forth, with knee lifts,
swift turns, and a final heel tapping.
"If you take some lessons," Menchu says,
"we can dance together at Feria."

The weeklong fair in April is
world famous. A mini-city of tents,
casetas—decked with streamers,
paper lanterns, set off by thousands of
multicolored lights—owned by
prominent families who comprise the
by-invitation-only heart of the festivities.
Because I know Menchu, I enjoy Feria
not as a gawking picture-taking tourist
but from the inside, as a participant.

Every afternoon features a parade
of prancing Arabian thoroughbreds.
Men and women ride by in formal habit—
tightfitting bolero jackets, white ruffled shirts,

wide-brimmed hats, hand-tooled leather chaps.
Some spirited females in flounced
flamenco dresses, low-cut in the back,
ride sidesaddle behind a dashing escort.
On occasion a couple stop at a caseta
for a friendly stirrup cup of *fino*.

Open-air ornate carriages promenade
the boulevards. A pair of coachmen
in swank livery guide a four-in-hand
of beribboned horses, a bevy
of Cinderellas in flamenco regalia,
flowers in their hair, hand-painted
silk Manila shawls on their shoulders.
The carriages pass to and fro
so they can see and be seen—
high society Seville on display
in all its pride.

That night, a half-bottle of Tio Pepe
in hand, I arrive at Menchu's caseta,
green-and-white-striped canvas outside,
lined with chairs for singers, dancers,
guitar players. In the rear a table of tapas.
Menchu is resplendent in her red dress
with white poka dots, frills on her sleeves,
formfitting at waist, hips, and thighs,
then flaring out at the bottom with tiers
of flounces to her high-heeled shoes.

Her black hair, pulled back in a low bun,
is crowned by carnations. One corny
song we dance to still echoes in my mind:

"You are my cross," the line repeats
three times, "and I carry you / just like Jesus."
My lessons in street clothes don't
prepare me for the erotic power of
a real sevillana. Swirling skirts brushing
my legs, fingers floating, eyes flashing,
Menchu is simply enchanting.

This romantic moment isn't going places.
Engaged since sixteen, Menchu will marry
her sweetheart. I meet my Catalan wife
Roser in Santiago de Compostela, destination
of many a weary pilgrim. We wed
in Barcelona, made our home in Maryland.
Now eighty, I well remember Feria
but not one step of the sevillana.

Picking Olives in Andalusia

Olive groves reach all the way
to the Sierras in the hazy distance.
Santos parks his *Dos Caballos* near
a laden tree and we get to work.
I am recruited for the risky task
to clamber up the trunk, ease out
on a limb, pick and toss them down.

Barbara and a few of her Sevillian
friends set up two ladders
and string a tarp between them
where the accumulated weight
of ripe olives creates a basket.

It seems that this ancient tradition
has an erotic dimension. Only men
climb the trees and pick the fruit.
They "throw down the seeds" to
the waiting women below, who wear
long pants beneath their skirts.

Picking olives is a skill
I am far from mastering.
With light fingers you caress
branches, careful not to break
tiny leaves and delicate twigs
needed for next year's crop.

At lunchtime we feast on
fresh bread, aged Manchego,
and of course some select olives,
drink *fino* sherry from Jerez.
The conversation of the women
in keeping with the occasion
is laced with sexual innuendo.

They ask Paco, a small gentle man,
if he ever married. "I have not,"
he replies with great formality,
"had that honor." When he walks
away, one of the women nods
after him and says, *"Uno y medio,"*
and they all burst into laughter.

Maro

1

Every day the sea is a different
shade of blue—turquoise becoming indigo,
aquamarine, cobalt, navy, azure.
At crack of dawn perturbed roosters cry,
clacking cloven hooves of bleating sheep,
gray coats the color of local stones,
and goats—a long rope trailing from a foreleg,
low-slung udders tolling from side to side—
led to pasture in the nearby mountains.
Each morning a different woman in black,
(one bucket, one brush in town) whitewashes
the walls of her house, while another (broom
of straw, plastic dustpan) sweeps the street.
A lean bare-chested man shovels manure
from mat baskets drooping down the back
of his horse, who farts loud and often,
then spreads it across his planted fields.
By afternoon it is too hot to work
or walk the streets. People stay inside,
take a nap or gather at El Guapo,
the town bar. The good-looking owner
calls me "Señor Tinto." "You will notice
people here have similar faces,"
he tells me, "because we're related:
Todo el mundo son parientes."

2

Maro at night is another story.
The sun sets prismatically on the sea,
a pink glow lingers, suddenly it is dark,
streetlights come on, women sit in doorways,
a constant commentary with neighbors
in loud, throaty voices; the men return
to the bar, discuss crops, weather, soccer,
raucous cries rising with each toast;
children playing games after midnight
make the most noise of all. No wonder
houses lack glass windows: these ear-
splitting sounds would shatter them.
One young girl toots a horn incessantly,
delighting all save one American
sitting on his balcony, sipping wine,
watching the moon over the mountain
emerge yellow-orange, twice as big as
expected, the face unmistakable:
lopsided grin, tilted Picasso nose,
deep-set eyes, inadequate round forehead
brushed by dark gray clouds, yet casting
enough light to reflect off the water
designing the sea in intricate patterns
of pale illuminations, purple shadows.
A welcome breeze rustles sugarcane stalks
offering an elusive promise of sleep.

Balcony of Europe

From a terrace in Nerja
a Mediterranean twilight
settles over the dwindling
waves of the sea, the last
waterskiers scud to shore
in a flurry of spray, causing
bikini-clad girls catching
the fading rays to squeal
in delight. Store shutters
clatter open to welcome
an evening promenade
featuring entire families,
arm-in-arm courtships,
and a staccato of hands
clapping flamenco in a bar.
As I sip my *granizado*
in the far distance I watch
the sun climb the mast
of a yacht whose bright
sails slowly darken until
the flag at the top briefly
glimmers. Behind the town
one by one lights of white-
washed mountain villages
punctuate the dark below
clusters of stars suspended
in a cloudless night sky.

Swatting Flies in Spain

Unless you find a drunken one
the hand is slower than the fly—
to kill the little foot-rubbing,
head-buffing, skin-walking,
insidious, pin-pricked,
come-from-behind, briefer-
than-a-buzz bug fuckers,
you've got to catch them
in mid-flight, slapping
quick hands together
at the precise spot
in the anticipated air
where they'll launch
ass-backwards from
the kitchen table.
The executioner simply,
simultaneously applauds
himself as the black spec
of death spirals to the floor.
Sweep it up later. First
wash your dirty hands.

Topless Beach

Quick green lizards dart
back at my step
as I walk down the zigzag path
terraced with tomato patches.
Today I'm sad to find
I have the beach to myself—
last night the movie crew
pulled out, abandoning
three sagging bamboo huts
and a tangled nest
of uncoiling purple film.
No loss there. But where
are the two German girls
whose stout Teutonic breasts
could always rouse me from
my dismal swamp of self?
I loved to watch them wade
into the hungry surf—
hands cupping breasts
to shield them from the waves—
it wasn't hard to taste
the salt tang of their flesh.
Now from the blue-green sea
a man in a black mask rises,
lifting impaled on a metal spear
a limp gray octopus.

Puerto de Santa María

Family restaurant with green doors,
fat father yelling at fatter sons
to clear more tables for restive locals
plus a few foreigners like me.
"Wait a minute," one son tells a group
in three languages. *"Qué desastre!"*
eyeing piles of dishes higher
than his head. In the kitchen
two even fatter women sweat
over steaming pots the size
of cauldrons. A rooster struts
across the sawdust floor,
cackles an irate commentary.
Father and sons keep shouting,
a beggar's opera awash in arias.
As the need is sorest food arrives:
tall glass of gazpacho, fried sardines
fresh from the Mediterranean,
sliced kidneys in a sherry sauce,
lamb shanks in a wicked stew,
wine named for a bull's blood,
pastry for the arm of a gypsy.
A meal worth the wait, a real find,
at a fraction of a fine restaurant
in Seville. For the best eats
look to the girth of the cook—
I learned that in Andalusia.

Paseos

In the evening the town
gathers at the fountain,
walks the shaded square
fronting the church.
Young girls in white dresses
scatter rose petals
from silver dishes,
followed by a band of boys
in soldier uniforms
carrying wooden guns,
banging loud drums.
Teenage girls in brightly
colored dresses link arms
and promenade,
boys eye their passing,
a few follow them,
make sassy remarks,
note which girls laugh.
Old women sit in doorways,
sad eyes and silence,
black dresses blending
into darker shadows.

Palma del Río

On a drive from Seville to Córdoba
beside the slow-moving brown waters
of the Guadalquivir, I stop to see
the castle at Almodóvar del Río,
whose crenelated walls and towers
crown a steep hill commanding
the river valley. Unfortunately
it is privately owned, not open
to visitors, thus I can make
an extra visit on my trip.

For no particular reason, I choose
a nearby pueblo, Palma del Río.
As I walk a cobblestone street,
dilapidated wall on one side,
the red-brick Baroque steeple
of the Church of the Assumption
ahead at the heart of the town,
I experience an eerie sensation
I've never felt before or since,
as if the air is thick with ghosts.

Years pass before I learn the story
of the town, best known for El Cordobés,
the celebrated bullfighter born there.
Before the Civil War, almost every male
a dirt-poor peasant doing seasonal work
for one of three wealthy landowners,
the daily pay a *duro* (five pesetas),
not enough to feed a family—the women
nurse one child and expect the next—
and even drinking water has a price.

Don Félix owns the prime bottom land
between Seville and Córdoba, olive groves
reaching the Sierra Morena. His prize
possession a herd of Saltillo fighting bulls
running free to graze a vast pasture
until their fearsome power could be
displayed in the bullrings of Spain.
Palatial homes in Seville and Palma,
his favorite car a big black Cadillac.

In 1936 the anarchists take over Palma.
They are poor because others are rich,
without bad laws people would be good,
if landowners were gone, all troubles
would be over. They burn down
the town's four churches and two convents.
After priests and nuns are dragged away,
statues smashed, paintings slashed,
a few peasants, before torching an altar,
cross themselves.

Juan de España, a mattress-stuffer's son,
runs the Revolutionary Committee.
To feed the local folk his men ravage
Don Félix's estates, stashing plunder
in the town hall, slaughtering prize bulls
each day, most residents get their first
taste of beef. The "bourgeoisie," forty-two
in all—café owners, doctors, taxi drivers,
vets, a lawyer, a druggist, a midwife,
a barber—are shot in the cemetery.

Then the tide turns, Franco's forces close in.
Town after town along the river is taken,
refugees speak of bloody reprisals.
Don Félix in his black Cadillac leads
the column into Palma. Juan de España
and his anarchists have fled, hundreds
of peasants are forced to line the wall
by the road to the church. Don Félix
struts past, looks each one in the face,
orders some to form a shorter line.

The men in the longer line pity
those selected to suffer for the sins
of the town: killing the priests, nuns,
and the people who had some cash.
Yet it is the slaughter of his bulls
that incenses Don Félix. He pardons
the shorter line, *"Al corralón"* (to the corral),
he shouts at the others, where a machine gun
mows them down, pausing to truck bodies
to a freshly dug trench in the cemetery.

At the time of my visit I notice
a rubble-strewn field next to the church.
Strange, since I am standing in the center
of town. No sign proclaims the site
of tragedy, the several hundred who died
for savoring a juicy steak. A plaque
does commemorate those who sided
with Franco, drew a salary, their graves
are shaded by eucalyptus trees.

Neither the anarchists who kill them,
nor Don Félix for his fell revenge
on the local peasants he has
condemned to poverty, are brought
to justice, if justice applies in this.
When I read of these atrocities
I realize what those ghosts whisper
to me at the Church of the Assumption
is that the story of Palma del Rio
is the story of the Spanish Civil War.

A Trip to Madrid

At Zaragoza a man boards
the train, cap pressed to chest
he tells his hard-luck story
before walking down the aisle
with his hand out, steps off
at the toot, crossing himself
as he passes by our coach.

The train rolls through golden
wheat fields in Aragón, here
and there a brown village huddles
on a hillside beneath the ruins
of a decapitated castle that once
defended, still crowns, the top.

Crossing an ancient bridge I see
a shepherd leading black goats
up the shining white stones of
a dry riverbed. *"Hola, primos,"*
a child pipes up at every stop
until his mother lightly pats him
and says, "Not yet."

                          In Madrid
the window is still missing on
the tenth floor of the Ministry
of Defense, shattered glass
on the street where ETA fired
a rocket attack from a truck
was cleaned up weeks ago.

Jerez de los Caballeros

In Extremadura life indeed is extremely hard.
On the road through the cork forest, the red velvet
of stripped trunks evokes wounded soldiers
after a battle. As I near the town at dusk
I'm slowed by a man on a horse and a woman
walking behind, a wooden pitchfork on her shoulder,
holding the horse by the tail. Then comes a woman
in a black babushka leading two oxen pulling
a cart piled with grass, her husband riding on top.
A church spire, a circling stork, I am there.

The men at the bar in the town square
treat me to a glass of wine. It's good manners
to treat back, but they're eight and I'm
hoarding my pesetas for a trip to Portugal
to renew my visa and I lack enough Spanish
to explain. I do manage to ask for a place
to spend the night. I am escorted to a house built
into the side of a hill—my room is up a slanted
hallway. When I wake to pee and stumble
out my door I feel far drunker than I am.

Since the town is known as the birthplace
of conquistadors, in the morning I want to see
De Soto's house. People point in various directions
until a woman at a window says, "He means
the old one," not current residents of the town.
His home is small, marked by a plaque, that
of Balboa is about the size of a one-car garage.
As I drive away I find myself stuck behind a man
on a donkey headed down the mountain
toward his terraced fields of wheat and flax.

Leaving Seville

I live in barrio Santa Cruz,
on a street named
Consolation, near the corner
where *Agua* meets *Vida.**

We sit side by side
and talk face to face,
clearly it will be
a long way to her lips.

Tonight I veto kisses
and vote for solitude,
tomorrow I'll stand
before a shut door.

The bartender puts
chairs on top of tables
but I won't pay up
or stop laughing.

Who knows where I'm going,
I forget where I've been,
like the river I'm flowing
I'll not be back again.

* Calle Consuelo, Auga (water), Vida (life)

II

Barcelona Posa't Guapa

Plaça Reial

for Paul Blackburn (1926–1971)

The palm trees are still there, Paul,
people of all ages pack the stone benches
by the fountain and in the evenings stroll
across the square under the spiky, vaguely
threatening wrought-iron streetlamps
designed by a young Gaudí. Couples
still carry babies in their arms
and long-legged women of the kind
you kept your eye on are often seen,
nowadays from all parts of the world.

Plaça Reial is an enclosed surprise at
the heart of the old city, an arcaded square
accessed by alleys adjacent to the Ramblas,
its high-shuttered apartments on all sides
contain a Parisian flavor. Like Washington Square
in the seventies, it was once the den of drug dealers,
prostitutes, pickpockets, and purse snatchers.
A seedy ambiance adds spice to its charm,
but now the word is *Barcelona Posa't Guapa*
and the facades are freshly restored.

It's no secret from the tourist hordes,
tables from many cafes fill the arcades
and spread into the square. Your favorite bar,
the Glorieta, is long gone, Paul, along with
the organized waddle of the waiter you evoked
in "The Touch" who remembered you after
many years and tapped your shoulder.
When he died you realized you never
knew his name and that we don't need
to know people's names to love them.

Roser Plays the Field

at a Costa Brava Beach

Germans do gymnastics
in the sand, scant swimwear
packs the crotch,
blond or auburn hair
long, not tangled,
blue eyes curious, direct.
They ask the girls
what classes they take,
talk about work,
lack nerve to request
a proper date. French guys
dress with studied
decadence, sidle near,
whisper propositions,
move tentative fingers
up and down a girl's arm,
take offense at any refusal
to give a name. "Why not?
You're a woman, I'm a man."
British boys are nervous,
reserved, look askance,
with an air of mystery.
The girls make a point
to flirt with them, cozy close,
ask for a light: *"Tienes fuego?"*

Alas, few sparks fly.

Roser

All I do is reach
across the table
and touch your cheek
to make you smile,
and if I put
my right arm
around your waist
your left circles mine.
This is called
falling in love,
pressed lips
in dark corners
and the promise
of more. Maybe
a shared place
in the summer
a quaint pueblo,
flowered balconies,
whitewashed walls,
nearby mountains,
and an easy
walk to the sea.

The Gift

Roser's mother Antonia isn't
close to her mother-in-law
Conchita, who feels her son
has married beneath him.
Once when Antonia praises
Conchita's emerald earrings,
she replies she will never
get them, they are going
to her daughter Esther.
Antonia has no such desire,
her remarks miss the mark.
When Conchita dies, after
Antonia has cared for her
late in life, the earrings
do go to her daughter.
Years pass, Esther, fifty-six,
is dying of cancer. One day
Roser and I visit her
posh apartment for snacks
and sherry. As we leave she
gives Roser a present. In the taxi
we unwrap it and find
Conchita's earrings as well as
her diamond wedding ring.

When Roser shows her mother
the gift, Antonia cries.

María

1932–1964

Back when French existentialists
rule over the songs, there is a bar
in Barcelona that affects an existence-
precedes-essence air. Aunt María
takes Roser, tells the waiter to think up
something a little girl might like. She
wants a milkshake but he brings
some flat soda water while María
downs drink after mixed drink then
kneels before Roser, with an awful
urging in her voice vows that
next to her own children she is
the thing in the world she loves
most. She is serious, her eyes
look hungry enough to devour her—
frightening, how serious she is.
Next two slick lounge lizards
try to pick her up, and, against
all odds, she brushes them off.

Blaming constant headaches, she
pops aspirin like candy, sips
magnesium as if it were Coke.
Once she chugs a dozen bottles
of Orange Crush then, given one
on the house, she drinks it too.
Often she wears a black turtleneck
and tight black slacks that set off
her slim figure and dark hair.
She sings and dances to the songs
of Johnny Hallyday, the little lion,
who despite his name is French.

Sometimes she straps bongos
to her waist to caress the calypso
rhythms of *Daylight come / and
I wanna go home.* Her ex-con
husband absconds to Boca Raton,
she and her boy and girl rely on
the wealth of her indulgent family.

María goes to sleep at dawn, wakes
in midafternoon. Every experience
forms part of an unfolding drama
where she is always center stage.
Her doting mother praises her capacity
to absorb life through every pore, how
she can have any man she wants.
Once she goes missing and is found
dead drunk by a railroad track not far
from a gypsy camp. Her doctors make
differing diagnoses: one says paranoid,
inclined to nymphomania; the other
declares her a spoiled brat. Both
recommend a period of observation
at the clinic. She develops a tan
from playing tennis, then is sent home
for seducing the gardener, a truck driver,
three patients, two nurses, and a therapist
specializing in sexual disorders.

Francesca's Secret

Whenever Roser's grandmother Francesca
loses something she chants three times:
 Devil, I give it to you out of pity.
 If you don't want it, give it back to me.
And often, afterwards, she finds
the missing thing. When Roser asks why
she sings those words, Francesca looks
surprised. Everyone knows the Devil
doesn't want anybody's pity, so he
surely will return the tainted gift.

Roser's father gets upset with these
superstitious mumblings and, when
he can no longer contain himself,
bursts out about such old-fashioned
nonsense. His scientific explanation:
the chant helps his mother-in-law
to clear her head and concentrate on
where she left the missing object,
but Francesca merely shakes her head,
for it is perfectly obvious only
the Devil can account for how
lost items turn up found.

The Little Barber at War

Catalonia, 1936–1939

Roser's Uncle Joan* is called
"the Little Barber" since as a boy
his father teaches him to cut hair.
At the start of the war, Anarchists
vowing "death to the bourgeois"
turn the shop into a cooperative,
pay his father a salary. Joan joins
the fight against Franco. Because
he is nearsighted, his family hopes
he might avoid the Front. Asked
to read some letters, he says they
are blurry. "You'll see the Moors
well enough once they come after you,"
the doctor warns and soon Franco's
Moroccan troops *are* after him.

          One day his unit
is bombed by a Messerschmitt.
Joan, on his back in a trench,
catches a glimpse of the pilot's face.
After two attacks, a soldier stands up,
mocks the pilot for dropping his load
short on the initial dive, long on
the second. The third doesn't miss.
Once it is over a few men, unaware
they are hit, spring to their feet
then suddenly collapse, dead.
Joan sees a large shell smack
the muddy ground, bounce over
his head, then explode further
down the line. His friend Esteve,

crouching nearby, vanishes. Not
a trace left. Joan never forgets
the cries of the dying nor the sight
of the river Ebro running red.

After his unit surrenders he is sent
to a concentration camp in Alicante
where a vain Franco captain takes him
under his wing as his personal barber,
feeds him steak and fries instead
of the usual sardines. Joan's father,
an agnostic, has made a promise
to the Dark Virgin of Montserrat
if his son returns home safely
he will make a barefoot pilgrimage
to her shrine up on the mountain.
And so he does. Roser assumes
her gentle, under-five-foot-tall uncle
was in the auxiliary services,
a stranger to front-line combat.
He is eighty-one, in the last year
of his life, when he finally tells us
how his trench was bombed, killing
his comrades, many still teenagers.

This poem is about bearing witness
and respecting silence.

---

* *Joan,* a man's name in Catalan, is pronounced the same as *Juan* in Spanish

In the Pyrenees

If you hanker for Romanesque
churches with sculpted portals,
cloisters where every column
is topped by fine-crafted figures
animating cold stone in scenes
from a distant Medieval world
where sacred and profane,
saint and drunken reveler,
meet face to face—then drive
to the Valley of Aran, remote
a thousand years until a tunnel
cut through rugged mountains.
In each town an ancient church
earthbound by gray granite,
a bell tower rising to the sky.
Above the altar a flaking fresco
of a seated Christ *Pantocrator*
holding the world in one hand.

In the valley you confront
tortuous drives to rustic towns
clinging to its flanks, narrow
streets lead to arcaded plazas,
one dead-ends at a fancy spa.
Although a pricy Parador serves
swordfish tasting like cardboard
dipped in orange juice, Catalan
cuisine is justly celebrated.
In the tiny town of Meranges
we dine at Can Borrell, a five-
star restaurant tucked away
at the end of a scenic valley.
I have black sausage and beans,
Civet d'Isart [venison stew],

a Raimat cabernet. The chef's
grace note, sautéed mushrooms
plucked from the mountainside.

If you travel in the Pyrenees
and savor good food, prepare
to change plans and stay another
night (my choice rabbit in pear
sauce), vow to return next year.

Taking Pictures

1 Andorra

Walking back country roads
of Andorra we see a couple
in peasant garb threshing hay.
I can't resist taking a picture.
When the man notices, his eyes
shine with rage. Stepping
forward he swears, "I shit
on God! if you try to use
that machine I'll stick you
with this," shaking a pitchfork.
He speaks a Catalan dialect.
I don't understand a word.
Roser, a Barcelona native,
tries to annul the death sentence
with a smile, assuring
them we mean no harm.
"The mountains, the mountains,"
his wife says, waving behind her,
offering us at a way out.
"They are very pretty."

2 East Berlin

The wall is still standing
and white crosses mark
the spots where people seeking
to escape were shot. I get
in trouble by snapping a picture
of Russian soldiers in uniform
gathered beneath one of those
grotesquely huge statutes

of Heroic Soviet Warriors
cluttering that side of the city.
A soldier arranging a group
portrait of his comrades sees me,
demands my film. We argue
with incomprehensible words.
One drunken fellow, seeing I am
no spy, only a tourist, jovially
intervenes, enables my escape.

3 Teba

I make a day trip with
Scottish friends from Seville
to visit an Andalusian pueblo
that overlooks a vast plain
where in 1330 an expedition
of crusaders from Scotland
besieged the castle at Teba.
The Moors sallied out
for a ferocious counterattack.
In the heat of the running battle,
James Douglas threw the preserved
heart of Robert the Bruce,
kept in a small silver casket,
at the enemy, shouting,
"Forward brave heart
as thou wert wont to do!"
The Scots charged, suffered
heavy losses, won the day.
Afterward, they recovered
their precious relic. Positioned
by a dilapidated castle wall

I take a picture of some men
dragging a metal detector
across the nearby grounds.
Once again an angry man
wants my film and again
I refuse. He glances at
my well-built friends; I keep
my camera. Later I see the light.
They are stealing antiquities
to sell on the black market—
I am no cop, just another thief.

The Referendum

Barcelona: 1 October 2017

At St. Thomas More high school—
the martyr executed by his king for
being true to his conscience—working-
class folk from other parts of Spain
line up to vote when someone shouts
"Here come the forces of occupation"
decked out in otherworldly riot gear—
visored helmets, bulletproof vests, clubs.
Sledge hammers smash the glass door,
police meet passive resistance, everyone
sits on the floor with hands up in silence.
They confiscate every scrap of paper,
grab ballot boxes, march out
in triumph. The people on the floor
applaud; the rude intruders
are hoodwinked—the boxes stuffed
with blanks, real votes concealed
for counting later. "We're tired
of all this Franco nonsense," a woman
cries out. "We want something else,
something better. We want
a real democracy."

Aureli's Funeral

He dies suddenly, cancer
of the lungs, although the way
he spews blood across the room
makes them think it might
have been his heart.
He smoked, like most Catalans,
spent his life breathing the bad
Barcelona air. Once he showed us
Roman ruins near his summer home.

The parking lot beside the dry
riverbed being turned into a highway
for the Olympic games is littered
with condoms. Two widows
show up for the official service
and only the husband in the box of
polished wood holds his tongue.

Outside I watch a trim young man
in skintight T-shirt and shorts
working hand over hand
up and down the huge stones
of a church tower. He uses
a small black bag strapped
to his back to dip his fingers
and select the next grip.

    The public building,
designed to process multiple funerals,
has twenty-nine rooms for close
relatives to gather and receive what
consolation can be offered while
packed together in a cramped space.
Everyone talks at once, somehow
the words seem to help.

Some Sayings

1 Going topless

In Seville bad behavior is called *feo* (ugly);
in Barcelona good behavior is *maco* (pretty),
aesthetics and ethics mix. Take topless bathing:
on the beach women who expose unsightly breasts
are frowned upon, shapely women browning
in the sun meet with hearty approval.
In America going topless is morally wrong—
no one should do it—or morally right—
every woman should go topless.

2 On stupidity

The king, the joke goes, is given two gold medals,
one for being stupid, the other in case he loses the first.
They say the Guardia Civil always walks in twos
because one can read and the other write.
Fools say foolish things, the saying goes,
and the clever do them.

3 On soccer

When neither team aggressively advances the ball
the crowd shouts, *"Que se besen"* (let them kiss).
Antonia, watching such a match where each
team plays footsie with itself and no one
is willing to make a risky move, glances at the TV
and remarks, "They promenade in the pasture
killing flies with their tails."

4 On religion

Priests are the only persons in the world
that everyone calls father,
except their children,
who call them uncle.
Menos monjas y más brujas
the graffiti on the wall reads:
"Fewer nuns and more witches."

On Pets

Newlyweds in search of a place
to live, his Barcelona bride
sees a "No Pets" sign, bursts out
laughing—it seems *pet,* in Catalan,
means fart, and the country has
a long folk tradition of anal jokes.
A peasant in a red Catalan cap,
or **barretina**, breeches down,
squats over a cone of crap
in a souvenir shop window.

On holidays this same fellow
appears in crèches for Christmas
stooping at the back of the stable
to heed the call of nature as
Jesus is born. Children smack
a yule log packed with toys and candy
while chanting, "Shit, log, shit,"
and at the Feast of Kings good
children are given sweets, bad ones
get *"caca i carbó"* (shit and coal).

A thirteenth-century ballad
celebrates a hundred noble ladies
who conquered becalmed waters
by filling the ship's sagging sails
with their synchronized flatulence.
Old Barcelona was bordered by
two rivers that were sewers
overflowing with human waste,
while Miró and Dalí and Gaudí
all feature excremental images.

Josep Pujol, *Le Petomane,*
appears in Paris music halls,
his final tooting: *"La Marseillese."*
If it's high up in a mountain,
Catalans sing, shit doesn't stink.
Rabelais flaunts the scatological,
as does Ben Franklin in his essay,
"Fart Proudly." The favorite line
from Dante of Italian schoolboys is
"He made of his rump a trumpet."

Pickpockets

Pickpockets feed on tourists,
vandals on motorbikes swoop
by an unwary person to snatch
a briefcase, a purse, a wallet
left on the roof as a distracted
driver bends to lock the car.

As I walk the Rambles
in Barcelona three gypsy women
rush toward me with hands out,
nudge me as they beg,
while one snatches my cash.

Waiting by the side of a bus
to retrieve my bags a man
abruptly bumps me, instinctively
I reach for my wallet, feel
fingers seeking my back pocket.

Some are stealthy, show a fine
persistence, carefully remove
the rear window of a car parked
overnight on the street, after
stealing whatever is visible,
leave the window unbroken
on the front seat.

                        In Seville
this happens night after night
to a visiting friend, even though
all valuables are safely secured.
A bold defiant demonstration
to show a car owner the night,
the street, and you belong to us.

Last Visit to Barcelona

A long-haired beggar
sprawls on the sidewalk
paralleling the Rambles
where packs of people
promenade day and night
placing in front of him
four tall plastic cups:
"Wine, Beer, Weed, Food."
A passing wag remarks,
"I don't see 'Cocaine.'"

A flush-faced drunk
in front of the main
government building
explains loudly to his
reluctant listener
a fervent conviction
that Núñez is a better
player than Navarro.

A small sign in the elevator
of our hotel reads: "There
will be no hot water
between 12:00 and 15:00.
Discuss the Discomfort."

III

Travel

Travel

Travel is the saddest
pleasure in the world,
moving at whim through
places we will never
return to, faces we
will never see again,
and words we do not
understand. We travel
to say we have traveled,
and as we go we squint
one eye, close the other,
and hold between us
and the thing we have
come to see a contraption
out of Plato's cave
(complete with its flash
and fire) so that when
we return to the place
we left from and throw
on the living room wall
the shadows of where we
might have been, we say,
"Look, that's me, with
the Parthenon on my shoulders,"
and, "Look, that's me again,
holding up that leaning tower
with one hand!"

The Perfect Shower

There must be a soft mat to step on
when you enter and exit and a rubber
nonslip one that fits the tub floor.
As you lift first one leg then the other
to step in and out of the shower
at least one bar should be firmly attached
to the wall, not of metal set at a slant
that is slick when wet and affords
no sure purchase. Since people die daily
from slipping and hitting their head
on the edge of the tub this lack
of safety planning is shameful.

On a lesser note place the soap dish
at easy reach of a person standing,
with a hole in the bottom for water
to drain thus keeping the soap moist
not soggy. This dish should be shaped
to hold soap, shampoo, and conditioner
securely, so that nothing can fall.
We all agree the faucet should clearly
indicate hot from cold and how to switch
the water from faucet to shower head
delivering a broad, soothing stream
from numerous tiny outlets.

There must be a ledge at the tub's top
to put each foot in turn as legs are scrubbed.
Turning off the water ought to be as easy as
turning it on, exiting as safe and convenient
as entering. The towel should be long, fluffy,
highly absorbent. It would be a most
satisfying thing to bathe in such a way,
alas, in my experience, the perfect shower
does not exist.

The George,
or Farewell to Merry Old England

The impeccably dressed publican
serves my shandy on a silver tray.
The bar's dark carved mahogany sheen
might inspire a violin-maker's envy.
The lone discordant note in this highly
civilized place, a drunk in the next booth
singing sailor ditties. "I say, mate,"
the publican softly says, "you've had
quite enough today. Time to go home."
Some soused muttering, followed by
a raucous song. The publican returns,
grabs the man's jacket, flings him to
the floor, kicks his face, breaks his nose,
leaves him weltering in blood. "Here. Here,"
Harold, my New Zealand friend, declares,
"you don't kick a man when he's down."
A code more honored in the breech by
these vehement regulars who as one
proclaim, "It's his pub and he can do
what he likes." Our best response is
to help the man to his feet, wipe blood
off his face, steady him out the door.
We prop him up against a wall,
offer to take him to a hospital—
but he wants no part of that.
Under a streetlamp we leave him,
singing.

On Hamlet

Hamlet, not Heisenberg,
discovers the principle of
indeterminacy—it's the key
to all the punning in the play,
elusive words won't stay put.
The meaning is not found in
what Hamlet will or will not
do next, but in what he will *say*.
It is his words, not his actions,
that matter.

        He wants to catch
the conscience of Claudius
to swiftly avenge the death
of his father, but his ever-
questioning mind changes
the consciousness of
his audience as they gaze
at the human condition
with fresh eyes. Then
the voice of Hamlet stops—
the rest is silence.

Mind the Gap

"Mind the gap," a canned
speaker cautions entering
the lift, which of course
can also descend.
This is London, where
minor dangers come
prefaced by hyperbole,
"a frightfully steep curve."
Yet "gap" is a kind
of understatement,
there *is* a deep drop,
an abyss, a rug that fate
can pull out from under
your feet. Best not consider
this matter too closely,
lest you find the abyss,
as Nietzsche warns,
staring back at you.

Saffron Walden

The town is mostly green,
the houses stone or brick,
some with steeply pitched
brown roofs of thatch.
It is quiet there—
but for certain nights
after the pubs close
when you might hear
the sound a man makes
when he's being kicked,
and next morning early
some woman will be out
sweeping broken glass.

It is lovely, really,
well-organized, with flowers
adorning every house.
There is even a village maze
laid out in ancient stones.

It might not be
a bad place to live,
only that nothing ever
happens there, except
in history, which you can
always read about in
some louder place
where there are, perhaps,
far too many people
and too few flowers.

Banksy's Prank

5 October 2018

Oh so poignant, so ironic,
a spray-paint and acrylic image
of a little girl's outspread hand
reaching for a heart-shaped balloon
eluding her grasp. No wonder
"Girl with a Red Balloon"
fetches a cool million pounds
at Sotheby's in London no less,
but as the auctioneer announces
"Going, going, gone"—poof,
the canvas scrolls down,
infiltrates the ornate gilt frame,
exits below in shredded strips.
The crowd collectively gasps.
A few cognoscenti see history
in the making, the shredding
integral to the work of art,
whose value has increased.
"The urge to destroy is also
a creative urge," posts Banksy,
the incognito artiste known
for subversive graffiti,
his images at home in the street
not over some fat cat's fireplace—
the check he does not shred.

The Berlin Wall

Even before I see the white crosses
placed where people who sought
to escape were shot, I hate that stark
proof of an Iron Curtain built with
blocks of cement. On a bus tour each
huge Soviet-style statue of heroic soldiers
is praised as if it were a work of art.
The Russians, I know, lost many millions
to defeat Hitler, but I'm talking about
East Berlin, a drab, depressing place
where the Cold War is no metaphor.

At Checkpoint Charlie, I exchange dollars
for mandatory-to-spend East German marks,
yet the few stores have nothing I want
except an art book with color illustrations.
When I ask the waiter how much for lunch,
he whispers broken English in my ear,
"It's twelve marks; you can have it
for three dollars." A mound of earth
marks Hitler's bunker, heart-high bullet holes
pock the sides of old buildings, where
the city's business center once stood
go-carts circle a dirt track.

I like best the Berliners' caustic wit,
gallows humor transforms oppressive
facts into spirit-lifting jokes. Our guide
in West Berlin debunks the famous sites.
Rebuilt and modernized, the city thrives
in a neon frenzy to sheer consumerism.

Yet I see hints of a darker side. Not that
anyone is anal, but my hotel bathroom
displays a set of tiny metal instruments
for inspecting your stool. When a soldier's
German shepherd ignores an order,
he slams it against a brick wall.
Returning to my room after midnight,
not a single car in sight, several people
stand at attention, unwilling to cross
the street until the light turns green.

That Summer in Paris

Hemingway/Fitzgerald Conference, 3–8 July 1994

Guy de Maupassant preferred the city view
from atop the Eiffel Tower where he
couldn't see the damn thing. We visit
Nôtre Dame as morning sunlight through
a rose window turns the transept
a ghostly blue, stroll bookstalls
along the Seine, gaze at garret havens
for starving artists. Sipping an aperitif
at Au Deux Magots I can picture
Jean Paul and Simone as their sycophants,
long-haired men, short-haired women,
swap *bon mots,* plot revolution.

First reception at Closerie des Lilas,
Hemingway's favorite bar, his son Gregory
denies his father liberated the Ritz
from Nazi occupation: "I've stayed there
and let me tell you it's not free."
Dinner is at the place Papa
and Scott met, a bar once called Dingo
now a small restaurant. Our hotel
an easy jaunt to the sidewalk cafés
of Montparnasse where the lost
generation of the twenties drowned
sorrows, courted the elusive Muse.

My favorite is Le Select, the last
old-timer left. My drink of choice
Pelford, a dark French beer with
a pleasant aftertaste. Our best meal
is Au Pied de Cochon in Les Halles,
multistoried wedding cake outside,

fancy bordello inside. The specialty
of the house, of course, is roast
pigs' feet in a hollandaise sauce,
also oysters fresh from the coast,
most memorable of all a bottle
of nouveau Beaujolais rosé.

The highpoint of the conference
at the Ritz on Place Vendôme,
a small bar, once for women only,
renamed to honor Hemingway.
Easy to spot his devotees: pot bellies,
full beards, rosy cheeks, part Santa Claus,
part satyr, deep-laughing beer drinkers.
The Fitzgerald coterie, notably thinner,
elegantly attired, most clean-shaven,
an occasional goatee or mustache,
cocktail in hand, intense discussions.

Budd Schulberg's hoarse stutter adds
a poignant note to his memory of Scott
as a gray ghost in a Brooks Brothers suit
and fedora. Sheilah Graham warns
that Scott can be a mean drunk,
yet to Budd he is a gentleman
of the old school, loyal and generous,
secretly subsidizing Hemingway when he
is down and out in Paris, convincing
Scribner's to publish him. By way of thanks,
Ernest caricatures Scott as a weak-
willed has-been in *A Moveable Feast*.

At the Key West home of Toby Bruce,
a mutual friend, Budd meets Hemingway,
who, drunk on rum, shoves his chest,
growls: "What the fuck do you know
about boxing for Christ's sweet sake?"
He wears shorts, fishing shirt unbuttoned,
ruddy face thrust forward. "Billy Papke?"
Budd knows he is the only middleweight
to knock out the great Stanley Ketchel.
Another poke in the chest. "Pinky Mitchell?"
Budd steps back, he was there when
Mushy Callahan took the junior welterweight

title from Pinky. Mushy gave young Budd
his gloves from the fight, for years they hung
over his bed. Another poke, pushing Budd
against the wall, seething. "Pete Latzo?"
He was a famous welterweight champion,
now a Teamster organizer in Scranton,
you can go visit him if you want.
Then Hemingway spins on his heel,
walks into the kitchen. Later Toby
sidles up and says, "Papa likes you."
Budd replies he admires his work,
will stay far away from the man.

To every writer there is a season,
Schulberg says in closing; he's known
some in the bloom of spring, others
in the winter of their discontent.
He had planned to praise the talents
of both authors equally, yet finally
he has to admit Scott was a prince,
Hemingway a bully and a bastard.

We savor Paris, learn from scholars,
are guests of Pamela Harriman at
the U.S. Consulate, yet I can't forget
Budd's stuttered words of truth.

How It's Done

Glance at the label
for age, locale, style.
Touch the bottle
for a temperature
not warm or cold,
gently swirl a dollop
in its shapely glass,
nose for aromas
of fruits, flowers,
herbs and spices,
lift the sample
by the thin stem
to the best light,
inspect for color
body, texture,
smile with a nod,
no need to taste
until the vintage
is properly poured.
Yet no matter
how skillful
the sommelier
a tear slides
down the bottle,
now the wine
begins to breathe.

A Brief Tour of Italy

1
Florence

Botticelli has it easy,
pastels on the walls,
blues and greens in sea,
sky, trees, beauty walks
the streets to avid eyes
or sits until the painter puts
his easel aside for the day.
David is still standing
in the Palazzo Vecchio,
still insouciant after all
these years, power
and repose with stone
in hand to make
vulgar giants regret
brutish behavior.

2
Venice

An otherworldly dream
rising from the sea,
a crumbling ruin
sinking in sludge.
A gondola gently rocks
on a slate-gray lagoon,
water laps stone steps
green with seaweed
and eroded by waves,
roses spill from a balcony,
a man is singing.

3
Rome

In a nerve-grating voice
an American woman
wonders how high
the Sistine ceiling,
what was there before
Michelangelo pulleys up
for his back-straining work
with palette and brush.
Her hubby matter-of-factly
estimates the project's cost.
Entering the Coliseum
the guide says, "Here
they fed a thousand lions
and tigers to hungry Christians."

All night lovesick cats
sing arias, marble fountains
caress themselves.
Streets narrow, serpentine,
buildings amber, salmon pink.
In Rome aesthetics rule.
Oh taste and see.

G.I. Joe in Naples, 1944

for John Horne Burns

1

Houses try to climb
the surrounding hills,
slide instead to the harbor
while in the background
Vesuvius fumes. Liberty Ships
cram the broad Bay of Naples.
Children eat black bread,
sleep on the sidewalks.
Limeys take tea at outdoor cafes,
watch streetwalkers jiggling
their wares. They call soldiers
"Joe," walk in pairs singing
"Chattanooga Choo-Choo."
Shoeshine boys near Via Diaz
and Galleria Umberto sell
Stars and Stripes for a dime,
their sisters for a dollar,
a stick of bubblegum.

2

It is one of those
war-torn love stories—
spirochete meets
penicillin and make
a separate peace.
In the clap shack
they shoot him up
around the clock—

jab each shoulder,
left butt, right butt,
day in, day out,
every three hours,
sixty shots
in eight days.

The Death of Marco Polo

A troubled priest kneeling
to administer last rights
admonishes Marco Polo
to confess his sins,
tell the truth about
his celebrated travels.
Everyone knows he has
exaggerated the facts,
told extravagant falsehoods
and fabulous tales of
golden cities in the East.
Surely he must set
the record straight here
before the eyes of men,
in the presence of God.
Marco motions the good
father to lean closer,
and, mustering what
strength he has left,
whispers loudly enough
for all to hear: *I have
not told the half of it!*

The Dutch Masters

A *trompe l-oeil* of dead game birds,
colorful plumage slightly fading,
eyes glazed over. A sunbeam
on the rim of a glass, ruby-red wine
glows from within as if radioactive.
The Dutch masters knew all the shades
of black, dark on dark defined an ultimate
penumbra with a golden hint of light
infiltrating the window in the corner
giving two ripe apples on a plate
of pewter a buttery-yellow hue.
Look closer: a small black speck
proves to be a fly symbolizing
the fact that in real life all of this
soon will rot, but in the painting
not yet—with luck, not ever.

A Soldier in the Great War

1 A Trip to Flanders

In Flanders the poppies bloom
blood-red, the cornflowers blue,
fields of wheat and barley
cover the hills where farmers
in season harvest their crops,
and milk cows graze on grass.

True, sometimes a plow exposes
bones of long-lost soldiers, a buried
dud explodes, on rainy days the smell
of rusty iron is strong, and we can see
remnants of zigzagging trench lines,
scattered ponds of old bomb craters.

Near a brick bunker by a canal
where doctor-poet John McCrae
did his life-or-death work,
identical white stone crosses
in neat rows honor the fallen
by name and date—when they can.

One is dedicated to a boy who
lied about his age, lived to fifteen,
but most repeat the same words:
A Soldier in the Great War.
The body, like thousands of
other war dead, has no name.

In the walled old weaving town
of Ypres, we walk beneath
a large marble arch carved
with the names of some
fifty-five thousand British troops
whose bodies are never found.

Names without bodies,
bodies without names,
this is what it meant to be
a soldier in the Great War.

2 Passchendaele

Passchendaele is a pretty town
with red-tile roofs and bright flowers
in window boxes. The paved
streets dry quickly after rain.

The battle plan is clear enough,
drive the enemy from the little village
on a nearby hill, until a steady
downpour transforms the ground

into a soggy morass where pressing
forward is out of the question.
Men bog down in thigh-high mud
and cannot move or be rescued.

Some die standing in place,
many of the wounded crawl
into shell holes for safety's sake
to slowly drown in rising water.

This battle in the mud slogs on
for months, corpses blown to bits
are hit again, spewing a putrid mist,
rain within rain, of human flesh.

Here in a flooded crater a flotilla
of bloated bodies, an empty helmet,
a boot that isn't, a medley of dead
soldiers from both doomed sides.

Several hundred thousand men die
to take, and lose, and take again
this village with a name the soldiers
cannot pronounce. Ypres they call
"Wipers," Passchendaele is simply
known as "Hell."

3 The General

He believes the Germans can not
withstand a thundering frontal assault
by a hard-charging line of cavalry,
each man brandishing a gleaming saber,
supported by shoulder-to-shoulder ranks
of troops advancing with fixed bayonets.

The moral force of such splendid courage
will unnerve the enemy, deflect his aim,
and cause a pell-mell retreat, a total rout.
Instead the foe keeps a steady pull
on machine-gun triggers, mows
his brave boys down in swaths.

The general is elated: how inspiring
it is to watch his gallant lads
maintain perfect discipline all the way
to the coiled barbed-wire entanglements
where like unstrung puppets they throw
frantic hands in the air and fall in heaps.

After losing half his force, not one
man reaches the German trenches,
the general describes the action as brisk.

4 No Man's Land

The notorious Ypres Salient creates
a bulge of several miles into German lines,
leaving the Allies exposed on three sides
to relentless artillery shelling. Soldiers

dig their own graves, the deeper the better,
and call them trenches. No safe place exists.
The two opposing forces are divided by
No Man's Land, an expanse of stinking mud

protected by barbed-wire entanglements
on both sides. All hardwood trees are
reduced to splinters, what then are the chances
in this forlorn waste space of a man's flesh?

When the troops are asked (ordered actually)
to up ladder and over the top into the thick
of it, they do as they are told. Not much
is required in the way of rehearsals.

All a man has to do is slog forward,
slip by some barbed-wire brambles,
and take out a cement block emplacement
harboring an enemy machine-gun nest.

Worse yet, at Ypres the Germans
first use chlorine gas, men foam
at the mouth, collapse in convulsions.
Livestock fall in the fields.

At the start everyone wants to get in,
as if the war were a swimming pool,
but only the rats, grown to a grotesque
fatness, prosper in No Man's Land.

5 Over There

When the poet-soldiers of England
venture forth to fight in Flanders,
they believe in honor and glory,
but the horrors of trench warfare
make them say goodbye to the
eternal verities—industrialized death,
an unspeakable wholesale slaughter
that drags on year after year,
neither side able to advance or willing
to retreat, is simply too absurd.
No leaders try to stop the folly.
As millions die so does the romance
of war, there are no heroes only
shell-shocked survivors. Our concept
of irony, Paul Fussell states, is born
on the Western Front. Yet wars
persist, the young still march off
as if mass murder makes sense.

6 Remembering the Great War

After the shell is planted
among us everything is roses
and poppies, I hope to never
again see such a blooming.

Skulls mushroom from muck,
rats' eyes take our measure,
bees flash by with a leaden buzz,
lice are our only lovers.

A gassed asthmatic, I keep
on the wall a fading map webbed
with lines, I run my fingers along
where friends were last seen.

Before the Revolution

for Turgenev

The bookish son, university-bound,
in work shirt and wire rims,
envies the booted serfs
who stand naked to the waist
swinging their scythes in the fields.
At night, unshaven, hostile, they
will lift up their heads and plot
murder in the dark.

Inside the house his father,
a superfluous man, drinks
vodka straight, fingers
a pawn and fails to find
a satisfactory move.
Sinking in self-disgust
he recalls how life
with its stern face
once asked him who he was.

The mother, aristocratic,
an ex-actress dressed
in white, keeps her chin up,
lets one bold peasant
kiss her delicate wrist.
She dreams of one good part
before she dies, of speaking
words like knives that set
everyone to weeping,
of the whole audience
standing, stamping, shouting,
as with open arms
she walks stage front
to receive their flowers.

Will Andrei Amalrik Survive Until 1984?

Guilty as charged, his deviant
ideology: that people have
a right to speak their minds.
Yet when absolute equality
(excluding a vanguard) is the goal
then a guillotine is the means
since anyone with eyes to see
must lose their head.

Before his show trial begins
the evidence is already known,
the verdict in. Neighbors
inform that strangers exited
his apartment carrying packages
of abstract paintings. How they know
what is inside the wrappings
a question not to be asked.

The tallest building in Moscow,
the joke goes, is headquarters
of the KGB, since from there
you can see all the way to Siberia,
where none of the millions shot,
starved, or dead of disease
receive a decent burial—
the ground is too frozen.

"I would prefer to be gagged
by the police, than to gag myself."
Andrei fears a country
where, when the cat bites,
the mice don't squeak.
Soviet rockets reach Venus,
in the countryside peasants
dig potatoes with bare hands.

The town's sole population
convicts and their guards.
In the penal colony the soup
looks like dishwater, a hint
of meat, a sliver of fish bone
that is an event. Andrei
on a hunger strike is force-
fed through the nose.

Guards prefer oblivion
by vodka, find pleasure in
beating their wives. A book
stripped of its covers, title page,
might pass for toilet paper.
A pencil peeled to the lead
and concealed in a cheek
the only way to write.

In 1970 he is in Moscow
when *Will the Soviet Union Survive
Until 1984* comes out in New York.
The Soviet state is on the verge
of an inexorable collapse,
a kind of "reverse Darwinism,"
an unnatural selection of the unfit,
will kill the system from within.

He feels like the first fish to warn
its fellows of poison water,
a world where social justice
means making sure nobody can
better themselves. A greedy elite
on top, passive masses at the bottom,
pretend pay for pretend work.
No one ready for multiple crises.

For exposing the Soviet Union's
dirty secrets, Andrei is labeled
a "social parasite," declared insane,
sent back to Siberia to tend cows,
finally allowed to seek exile
in the West where he teaches,
lectures, writes about Russian life,
carries his thesis like a torch.

Death comes to him in 1980,
on his way to a conference
in Madrid to review human rights
upheld by the Helsinki Accords.
His car swerves on a wet road,
is struck by an oncoming truck,
a metal shard from the steering
column punctures his throat.

Was it an accident? Or arranged?
His wife survives the crash,
thinks it deliberate.
The KGB wants him dead.
But then, he has always been
a sloppy driver. Eleven years
later the Soviet empire falls.

Woe to the prophet who speaks
a premature truth.

Odysseus Returns

1 Argos

Argos is a puppy when Odysseus leaves his home
to fight in the Trojan War, wander for many years
upon wine-dark seas, visit distant cities, delve
into the minds of many men, taste the favors
of women and goddesses.

When he returns disguised in beggar's rags,
the aged dog, left on a dung heap to die,
hears his master's voice, tries to wag his tail.
Seeing this, Odysseus strives to hide
his tears as Argos breathes his last.

2 Penelope

By day Penelope weaves a shroud for Laertes
she unravels by night thus keeping her suitors at bay—
just as she makes daily promises to the hundred men
to enmesh them in a subtle web until Odysseus returns.
She says it is for her father-in-law, but we know better.
It is for her long-lost husband, who for years has been
weaving and unweaving his extravagant way home.

When he appears as a ragged beggar crouched
by the fireplace the two exchange a warp and woof
of words creating a verbal tapestry that affirms,
in a way so sly it at first eludes her conscious mind,
who he is. Only when he boasts who made
their bed of mighty wood does she know
for certain her true love is back.

IV

Walkabout

The Wailing Wall

A tourist, playing it
safe, she takes a taxi
to visit the old city
although it is only
a fifteen-minute walk
to the wailing wall.

Young Israeli soldiers
finger machine guns,
glance warily about.
Jews from all over the world
cram paper prayers
into any available crack

in the stones. Here thousands
of years of suffering and anguish
are concentrated in one place.
Esther, without thinking, begins
to weep uncontrollably for
all the lost generations.

She came to the wall a tourist
and she leaves in tears.

Yes and No

When Ilse hands Rick the gun
he tells her "You'd be doing me
a favor" by pulling the trigger.
Instead, she flings herself into his arms,
confesses she tried to stay away,
if only "you knew how much
I loved you, still love you"—

the camera pans off to a phallic tower
while Rick bogarts a postcoital cigarette—
the question is did they play it again,
that fundamental love they had shared
in Paris since a woman needs a man,
a man must have his mate?

Neither the couch nor the couple
appear in disarray, barely a breach
in the conversation, just a discreet
ellipsis in the scene, thus the answer
is: yes and no—as you, the savvy
or naïve, like it—in Hollywood
everybody is allowed to keep
and eat their slice of cake too.

Rick reveals the truth:
"We'll always have Paris. . . .
We got it back last night."
She pretended to love him,
he tells Laszlo, to get that
ultimate McGuffin, the visas.
Neither man is fooled—who
loves whom doesn't matter if
saving the world is at stake.

A happy ending? Yes. And no.
Either way,
we'll always have *Casablanca*.

On the Nile

The headless houses of Egypt
haunt me. Sunbaked, redbrick
buildings standing by the Nile

ascend three, four, five stories
or more, top floors unfinished:
empty windows, often no roof.

Old or new, these drab structures,
browns darker than sand, eerie
sadness in blank windows,

resemble rubble-strewn ruins
of past bombardments. Yet
proud owners view vacant levels

as signs of hope. Sons will marry,
move in above them, sweep floors,
add windows, lay carpets, raise

a large family, perpetuate tradition.
In Cairo, however, a sprawl
of twenty-two million—traffic

a rugby scrum, each street
a logjam, chaotic architecture—
age-old rural practices yield

inhumane results. The *zabaleen,*
the people of the garbage—
dispirited, overwhelmed by

fields of sludge, hills of refuse—
no longer haul off the trash.
Forsaking peasant customs

that once made sense of
village life, people seek
sustenance in Islam.

From the air Cairo emits
the ghostly hue of the Sahara,
looks like a vast cemetery.

Hordes of people *have* made
homes of tombs, adding
packing crate or cardboard walls,

rusty iron roofs held down
by stones—it's called The City
of the Dead. All Egypt is a keg

of powder primed to meet
its match. In troubled dreams
I see those headless houses.

Queen Nefertari's Tomb

O excellent, I love long life better than figs.
—Charmian

1

To get from here to the hereafter
you must cross a river, if the water
is low a three-headed snake
with human feet will carry
your long slim boat over slime
to the far shore. Even Egyptian
pharaohs and their queens
live in homes of brick from
the mud of the Nile, seasonal
flooding creates a fertile plain
that sustains all the people.
When they die, however,
mummified royalty—
coffins of gold, granite tombs—
are buried in desert hills
to the West, where the sun dies
before rising in the East,
a place high, dry, remote.

2

Life is brief, my friend, afterlife
without end. No better way
to pass the time than doing
forever things loved best
on this earth. Here the power
of art comes in. Whatever
Egyptian painters depict on
doorways, walls, ceilings
will have eternal life.
Thus they repeat images
of favorite foods, drinks,
animals, birds, trees,
daily activities—
all they cannot leave
behind. Religion derives
from fear of dying.
The more life is loved
the greater the belief
death is not the end.

3

In the Valley of the Queens
we descend into Nefertari's
House of Eternity, eighteen steps
down each narrow corridor
to asymmetrical chambers
flanked by annexes off kilter
to fit the labyrinthine design
of turns and counterturns
that evokes the torturous path
the dead take to become
effective, blessed souls.
Proof of resurrection is how
the colors on the walls are
vibrantly alive—not "restored,"
but painstakingly cleansed
from millennial damage,
limestone salt leaching into
the paint. Mine eyes dazzle
at the brilliant mix: soothing blues,
luxuriant blacks, stunning reds,
vivid whites, the roof spangled
with yellow five-pointed stars.

4

Repeated hieroglyphics celebrate
Nefertari: beloved of Mut,
king's great wife, mistress
of two lands, embodiment
of beauty, true of voice,
great of favors, possessor
of charm, sweetness, love,
for whom the sun shines,
who satisfies the gods,
is justified before Osiris,
whose transformative power
the queen seeks. Dismembered
by his brother Seth, miraculously
reassembled and restored to life,
Osiris, god of the netherworld,
appears as a mummy, swathed
in white linen, hands crossed
over his chest, flail in left,
crook in the right, his face
as green as the vegetation
returning to life each spring.

5

Nefertari seated at a gaming table,
eternal life at stake, then as a bird
free to fly away if she wishes.
Next as a supplicant, kneeling
in a sumptuous white gown,
a red sash at her waist, hands
raised in homage before Osiris.
His wife Isis stands nearby,
her beaded red dress clinging
to her svelte form. She holds
a scepter in her left hand,
reaches out her right, bracelets
glittering at her wrist, gently
drawing Nefertari forward
to receive Osiris's blessing.
Though fearsome gatekeepers
bar the way—humans with heads
of lion, ram, bull, crocodile—
she speaks the proper names
at the right time, Osiris is pleased,
a goddess spreads her wings,
a priest dressed in a leopard skin
presides as Isis extends to her
the breath of life. Tranquility rules
in this last sepulchral chamber.
Even the jackal smiles.

The Women of Tehran

Before landing in Tehran
one by one the women
retreat to the bathroom,
remove their makeup,
put up their hair, hide
their leotards or miniskirts,
don black shapeless *chadors*.
Yet on the streets of the city
they stare in your face,
kohl shaping their eyes,
red lipstick, purple nails,
in spite of oppressive black.
Confronted with a camera,
they smile, sometimes pose.
At late-night private parties
they dress to the nines—
orange satin, heavy makeup,
luxuriant jewelry—dance
with abandon, flirt openly
with all comers. If Iran
is ever to break free of
the ayatollahs, these women
will surely lead the way.

Islamabad

Safe water for the wealthy,
the poor turn the tap,
not a drop, a death rattle

from empty pipes.
Tenement toilets leak,
wasting precious water.

Leaky toilets easy to fix,
a city inspector imposes
a fine to force repairs.

For owners it's cheaper
to slip him a little some-
thing to feed his family,

than correct the problem.
So toilets keep leaking,
the city loses revenue,

population grows.
Water trucks arrive
in needy neighborhoods,

supply below demand,
locals bribe drivers to get
water first. Corruption

breeds contamination,
people swallow water
unfit to drink, diseases

spread from shantytowns
to gated mansions.
This time hepatitis

killing rich and poor alike.

Afghanistan

Our troops in Afghanistan
are issued hip-waders
where there are no marshes,
a chain saw fit for logging
in a land bare of trees.
Their mission to kill the Taliban,
a name that means student.
To the commanders the war
is a box to check, a step
up the career ladder,
for soldiers it is one more
body bag to fill, another road
where bombs do not fall
from the sky but are planted
underground like monstrous
lethal blooms, or concealed
by objects that appear
harmless. The real mission:
chasing ghosts in the deserts,
ghosts in the mountains,
while those ghosts keep
our troops in their sights from
village roofs, roadside ambushes.
"Two to the heart and one
to the head," the joke goes,
a mission accomplished.

An Outpost of Allah

Beneath a relentless sun,
in a vast desert where only
the ruthless slack their thirst,
a desolate mud-brick village
surrounded by sand. The men
don turbans, carry AK-47s,
shoulder grenade launchers,
while veiled women,
babies in their arms, balance
large jars on their heads,
wash floors on their knees.
A place where inflation is
so bad it's cheaper to buy
in the morning and the word
for yesterday is the same
as the word for tomorrow.
Distance to the nearest city
measured in days by camelback.
Here the best way to survive
is expect the unimaginable—
worse case scenarios acted out
before your eyes. The key:
show no surprise, that draws
their attention and in a flash
what you dread most
could be happening to you.

A Night at Samarkand's Starless Hotel

for Robert D. Kaplan

If you need a wheelbarrow
to cart away the local currency,
you can draw conclusions. Forget
romantic notions about Samarkand,
city of rusted pipes, corrugated-
iron roofs, unpainted cement,
cinder-block facades, the whine
of diesel trucks. In the hotel
restaurant, such as it was,
five men at a nearby table
debate which country is best
for hijacking a plane. Two thugs
in tight-fitting body shirts
flex their biceps in the lobby.
Plaster peels from the walls
like the skin of a burn victim,
the lightbulb hanging itself
by a wire in the middle
of the ceiling doesn't work.
The air is mastered by a gag-
worthy odor of cigarette smoke
and diesel oil. Brown water
drops from the tap and,
naturally, the toilet won't flush,
rather it sighs, dribbling
an ineffectual stream.
The door's lock is broken.
The springless bed descends
down to the dusty floor.

In India

She remembers smoking opium
on the roof of the hotel, watching
a red castle glow in the sunset,
and how cattle press against
the crush of people in the streets,
along with lepers, beggars, and
one beautiful woman who lifts
her sari to squat and shit in the dust.

Strangely twisted trees that never
seem to grow and the large temples
where monkeys swing in the rafters,
chattering. In the backcountry
the guide points at the moon
and shouts "American, American"
until the peasants nod and stare
at her with utter disbelief.

Gandhi and the Robber

When the robber comes
you open the door,
provide food and drink,
turn over your valuables,
lament his malady.
His smile the wrong size,
eyes try to walk away.
When the robber returns
he is confused, doors
and windows unlocked,
replenished valuables
in plain sight. Seeing he
is armed to the teeth,
you weep with pity,
plead he cease stealing.
He takes what he wants,
leaving the door open.
In the village he is told
of your loving heart,
your charitable deeds.
He repents, returns
all your things, begs
forgiveness, asks
to learn a better way.
You help find him
honorable employment.
This is the blessed method.

In Quest of Yeti

for Bruce Chatwin

If you're inclined to look for Yeti,
aka the Abominable Snowman,
Kathmandu is a good place to start.
You'll need a Sherpa as sirdar (guide),
another to cook for the long trek
in the direction of Mount Everest.
On the way to the village of Thome
("Way Up"), you'll pass blue iris,
bare birch trees. Yaks and wild goats
graze on the mountainside. Some say
the Yeti have yellow eyes whose gaze
is lethal. Perhaps the creatures
are a hallucination caused by
the High Himalayan air or they arose
from our Collective Unconscious.
All we see are footprints too large
for any yak, blue bear, snow leopard—
the usual suspects—that the sun
melts before our baffled eyes.
At the top of the mountain we meet
a Scotsman who scoffs at the notion
of a Lock Ness Monster but believes,
with all his heart, Yeti is out there.

Japanese Watercolor

Our hold on this world,
the watercolor says,
is a thin thread.
What is more fragile
than a tree sketched by
a few lines? The unraveling
stream falls down
the gray mountain rock
by rock, while the poet
in his haiku hermitage
takes note of mist
rising from the valley,
birds fanning the air
with delicate wings
the texture of rice silk.
A bright, tenuous rope
of blossoms secures
the subtle composition
in a tranquil place.

How to Capture an Anaconda

Reach into the river
and grab the creature
behind the head.
If you fall in the water
and the huge serpent
wraps itself around you,
hold the snake's jaw
away from your face
with your right hand
while unwinding
the powerful coils
with your left because
if the snake tightens
itself around your chest
you will suffocate,
if you are squeezed
too hard anywhere
your bones will snap.
Break free of the embrace
and lift the snake
up into your boat.
Now cram it deep
into your capture bag
and with strong twine
tie a slip-proof knot.

Next row your boat
swiftly back to camp,
and get some rest.

Tomorrow
we wrestle crocodiles.

Incidents on the Ivory Coast

for Denis Johnson

A tensed rope across the road,
young men behind an oil drum
trailing anarchy in their wake
wave Kalashnikovs in our faces,
another checkpoint to pass
if our luck holds. The dilapidated
town piled with broken stones
looks a thousand years old.
When scrawny boys in shorts
fire real guns in the square,
everybody laughs. In this country
the courthouse, reduced to rubble,
often the scene of the crime.
The hospital—doctors fled, electricity
off, no medicine or clean water—
the place you go to die.

When the latest Big Man comes
to power, he butchers his predecessor.
A pistol to a victim's head, pulling
the trigger his idea of a good joke—
the funniest part, the poor bastard
shits his pants. You can be shot
if your radio is not on when
the Big Man boasts how UN
peacekeepers killed that day
"die easily." In the evening at
the lake beside his palace he
feeds live chickens to crocodiles.
"Everything is arranged," people
who survive say in consolation,
meaning, "Shit happens, accept it,"
but they will not be the ones
doing the arranging.

Growing Tomatoes in Nigeria

for Vicenç Bosch

The Nigerian diet consists of rice, a hint
of meat or vegetables, flavored by tomato sauce,
yet this stable is mainly imported from China.
Our friend Vicenç's Catalan food company
tills land for a tomato farm, employs hundreds
of women, pays a good salary. Most give
the money to their husbands. At least one
uses the cash to buy a new motorcycle
and a second wife. When the company digs
a well in the nearby village of Wara so nobody
has to walk miles for clean water, the headman
claims it as his own, charges a fee.

Beside the farm the company has a factory
to process tomatoes into paste. The fresh
economic activity arouses greed and envy.
Everywhere Vicenç goes he is guarded
by men carrying assault rifles. Thousands
of acres are tended and a bountiful crop is
ready to harvest. Out of the Niger state forest
sweep hundreds of Boko Haram bandits
on motorbikes to kidnap the European "experts"
and hold them for ransom. Four policemen
are killed, Vicenç and the other men flee.
The tomatoes are left to rot in the fields.

Should the company return? The factory
is still intact, the fields can be planted
again next year, but is this a governmental
conspiracy to compel more payments
for protection? Since Vicenç and his fellows
are forewarned of the attack he suspects

all this might be a vicious cycle to let
the government pocket more kickbacks,
Boko Haram launch more raids,
while the people of Nigeria never get
the cheaper tomato sauce they need.

Rimbaud in Abyssinia

Rimbaud writes all his poetry
before twenty. His secret way
to illuminate unknown worlds
the derangement of the senses.
High on hashish, he predicts
the future is already here,
the time of assassins has come,
his work as a poet is done.

Having seen enough, known enough,
had enough, he wants to change life.
Magus of quick getaways, he
leaves the Sabine suburban women
to sob, abandons the boring
bourgeois world of decadent France,
spurns European culture
for a hot African country.

"I shall have gold," he vows,
settles for being a merchant
dealing in bales of coffee, hides,
a stint at gunrunning, perhaps
dabbling in the slave trade—ivory
for ebony, as it is called.
Mean and stingy, his shabby
caravans traffic in failure.

Walking is his avocation,
to be footloose and fancy free
his credo, to leave one place for
somewhere else his incessant goal.

Imprisoned by his own rib cage,
conspiring his own hell, he thrives
on disputes, often takes offense,
loves to detest his enemies.

He lives in Harar, putrid place
of sunbaked clay, and takes on
local customs, pees crouching,
works like a donkey, submits
to an atrocious existence.
At thirty he looks twice his age.
"The world is vile," he concludes.
"As for me, I have loved a pig."

Skin cancer, oblivion near,
he sets out for Egypt, kingdom
of pharaohs for thousands of years.
High on a pillar at Luxor,
deep in the stone he cuts his name,
then goes back to France to die.
Often delirious, with no idea
who he is, what he has been.

One leg amputated, the other
obscenely swollen, his deathbed
at his miserly mother's farm.
Since Rimbaud has fits of spitting,
the priest, fearing profanation,
refuses holy communion. "When
you walk in the sun," he says,
"think of me under the ground."

Tout suite French critics make his case:
He gives up words to touch the raw
material things of this world.
A bitter, irascible merchant
in a sordid, exploited place,
he winks. No fall, his silence
is his highest achievement.

Are his words, his life, eloquent?
No poet writes like Rimbaud today,
but some have mastered the art
to be no one you'd want to meet.

Santo Domingo

In Santo Domingo a choice of pink,
green, blue, yellow, or orange shacks,
people, undaunted, are all smiles,
thriving on sunshine and sea breeze.
That night cars, boom boxes blaring,
are bumper to bumper to celebrate
the newly opened waterfront highway.
Women recline on hoods of VW bugs,
sip rum, hundreds dance in the road
under bright streetlights beside
docked freighters and cruise ships.

Next evening poets read while an artist,
inspired by the words, paints behind them,
the audience intently watches and listens.
At the end several stand, eagerly offer
cogent comments. Asked about
Columbus and the conquistadors
one female poet replies, "I consider myself
thrice blessed to have Indian, African,
and European mothers. Let the so-called
conquerors enjoy their victory and let
the so-called victims lament their defeat.
I stand aside from the controversies
and celebrate my mestizo heritage."

Yucatán

A Spaniard wearing heavy armor
in the hot sun stands in a longboat
and calls out to a naked native
on the shore, "What is the name
of this place?" and is told, "Ci-u-then,"
meaning, "I don't understand you,"
and Yucatán it remains—like *Indians*
and *America,* one more misnomer.

When Spaniards try to conquer the Maya
they have already, due to a long draught,
abandoned their vast temple complexes
to the inexorable advance of jungle
undergrowth and live in open-sided
palm-thatched huts in small villages.

The Maya repulse the early invaders
but in time are overcome. In 1562
a decree to stamp out all idolatry:
*We found a large number of books
which contained nothing to be seen
except superstition and lies of the devil,
so we burned them all, which they
regretted to an amazing degree
and caused them much affliction.*

Centuries pass before restoration begins.
Stone monuments by ingenious builders
revert to earthen mounds covered
by bushes, brambles, vines, and trees.
Aerial photos reveal extensive roads,
irrigation canals, and farmland to feed
many people. The unending labor of digging
and rediscovery continues, yet much
of Maya civilization can now be seen.

Chichén Itzá

From the arcaded porch of the Hacienda
we can see El Caracol (the snail) named
for its spiral staircase, whose dome suggests
an astral observatory. At the irregular-shaped
swimming pool, banked with a flower garden,
large iguanas laze on hot rocks in the sun.
Still as stones, nothing moves except
their eyes watching us in the water.
Hard to ignore iguanas not ignoring you.

The Maya discovered rubber, knew how
to volcanize it, played the world's first
ball games in walled areas twice as long
as a football field. A carved stone image
depicts a victor holding up in triumph
the severed head of a vanquished player,
blood streaming from his neck like snakes.

El Castillo, the tallest pyramid, is now
closed to tourists ever since a woman
fell to her death, but in those days we
can still climb the steep ninety-one steps
to the top to find a hut-like structure,
walls embellished with Mayan glyphs,
a carving of the plumed serpent,
and a distant view of other monuments
jutting above jungle cover. An older
structure inside this one has a jaguar-
shaped throne studded with inlaid jade.

Monkeys cavort in tall trees as we
follow the path to the Sacred Cenote
that sustained Chichén Itzá. All rivers
in Yucatán are underground. Rainwater
dissolves soft limestone, causes the surface
to collapse into sinkholes, the largest form
cenotes, deep circular pools connected to
rivers and caves. Swallows cry as they swirl
around the sheer rock sides, a soothing breeze
rises from cool water. The Maya believe
cenotes are a gateway to the gods, in times
of drought they sacrifice gold, jade, people.
I look down at the placid surface and wonder
how many human bones lie at the bottom.

Guatemala

In Guatemala City we're surprised by all
the young American couples at our five-star hotel.
Honeymooners, we think, until realizing
they're here to adopt a Guatemalan child.

We board a bus to Lake Atitlán, catch a boat
for Panajachel, are warned not to get too close
to Maya children in the village, don't touch
any faces or heads or reach out for a hug.

Several months before an American
woman in a remote village, falsely suspected
of kidnapping a child, is beaten into a coma
with clubs, machetes, and metal pipes.

The booming business in adopting babies
is unregulated, corrupt, rumors spread
of men in jeeps with tinted windows killing
children to harvest organs for transplants.

Smoking volcanoes in the far distance capture
the splendor of the land and its underlying threat.
Right-wing death squads have slaughtered
thousands of Maya in the highlands.

From the dock to the village we run
a gauntlet of people selling local crafts,
mostly brightly colored woven goods,
hand-made pottery, feathered Maya dolls.

At the open-air market in the plaza in front
of the original colonial church each product
is in place. The women all dress in traditional
huipil (shirt), *faja* (sash), and *corte* (skirt).

"You like shawls, *mamita?*" a tiny woman
with an intricately embroidered one asks Roser.
"Very cheap," she says and lowers the price,
but Roser has not come to haggle or buy.

Inside the church a wedding is ending, the couple
kneel at the altar then leave to offer tobacco
at a local shrine: *Maximón,* seated, shabby black suit,
black hat, big cigar in mouth, gun in left hand.

As we exit the church the small woman waits,
offers the lovely shawl for only five *quetzales,*
follows us as we stroll the market marveling
at people in their distinctive native costumes.

I sense the persistent woman simply wants
to give us the shawl, but Roser insists on paying
the original price. "Thank you, *mamita,*" she says,
folding her artwork. "Now I can go home."

The Shining Path

Lima waits—under rat-gray
clouds that bear no rain—
for an invasion of babies.
In a shanty desert of tin
cans and cardboard they
sharpen their sexual weapons.
The night sighs with orgasmic
war cries. Babies are bombs.

At dawn a ragtag tide
seeps down the dry riverbed
into the heart of the city,
submerging the markets, the park,
the plaza of San Martín.
This is a hell no Virgil
could guide a poet across.
For every patch of street
there are two pistols
and the stale air is thick
with the sweaty smell of greed
you could cut like a cheese.

In the tree-shrouded suburbs,
in the homes of the rich,
from behind bougainvillea walls
crenellated with broken glass,
voice tinkle like lost bells.
A guard dog patrols every garden.

At dusk in the garbage dumps
children waltz over rotten fish.
As the moon rises they will follow
the shining path out to the razor's edge
where a chill wind blows, primes
bombs, and the cries of babies
soar up like flames.

Bolivia

You arrive in a psychedelic bus
packed with chickens, two pigs,
and women wearing Bowler hats.
In the town square by the Market
of the Witches some boys
are kicking a deflated soccer ball
in the dust. The Andean air
is almost too thin to breathe
and *chicka,* the local moonshine,
is fermented by a hint of spit.
The men have black lung
from working in the tin mines,
green feet from stomping
coca leaves into paste to send
to that cocaine-sniffing colossus
to the North. After the Revolution
each family received some land,
then subdivided among his sons
when a father died. Now families
barely subsist on freeze-dried
small potatoes. The only solution,
some say, one more Revolution.

Vietnam

1

He is wading
in a swamp up
to his armpits at
the deepest part.
There are snipers
in the trees,
nearsighted, he
hopes, without
glasses, because
a man's head can
be a big target
when looked down at
by a sniper
in a tree.

2.

Butterflies flutter
above the bodies,
drawn by the smell
of blood.
Their beauty
among the swarm
of other insects
hard at work
is dreadful
to behold.

3.

It's spring.
The dead man's belly
bursts, a flower
blossoms. Who
knew as bombs fall
if birds sing.

4.

They tag him,
bag him,
big bird comes,
flies him away
in a cloud of dust.

Walkabout

When I kill the first
kangaroo you smile
and eat your fill. Then
I stick a hollow reed
deep into the drying mud
to bring you fresh water.
Lizards I kill with a spear
made by biting a yellow
sapling, bending it straight.
You swim naked in a clear pool
while I hunt for you,
bringing small birds and ground
animals. When we find
the deserted house, the graves
and torn posters, I bring
you water from the spring.
You take it as if it is your due.
The night after we find the road
I do my courting dance, white
paint on my face, yellow blossoms
in my hands, all in your honor.
You stay inside, your ear
to the radio, while I dance on
till the flowers fall. In the morning
you'll find me, a shamed warrior,
one with the breeze, turning
in the wind from a bare tree.

Easter Island

Who will decipher
the secrets of
the stone faces?
Who will tell
the tale of how
the short ears
slew the long ears
and smashed those
gods whose eyes
were open?

The monoliths line
the island's rim
looking inward at
the secret land.
They know what happened
in their honor—
bones upon bones
in volcanic caves
an epic song sung
by the oldest woman
in the only village
her fingers lost
in a cat's cradle
that controls how
the tale is told.

Cargo Cult

When John Frum comes in the war
he is just one more G.I. Joe.
They watch him go to the cooler,
take out a round shiny creature,
scalp it, drink its blood.
Then with one hand he crushes
its skull, tosses it away.

The natives of Tanna, converted
to Christianity, carry holy water
into battle, suspect the missionaries
tore pages out of the Bible
telling how Jesus was born
and grew up on their island.

John Frum comes with a surplus
of supplies, whatever the people
want they get—food, clothes,
medicine, better housing material.
Music plays from a little box
and everyone sings and dances.
John Frum makes a small flame,
smokes his pipe, and laughs.

Then John Frum and the big boats
and birds bringing good stuff
go away. He promises to return.
They clear an airstrip, erect a replica
of a plane, men in pants of red, white,
and blue, USA painted across their chests,
march in formation, do precision drills
with bamboo guns, turn a straw crank,
talk to a wooden radio. The origin
of religion is in their pure belief:
"John Frum, he come back."

Fossil Time

If the earth existed for one day,
at midmorning life emerges,
by lunch oxygen feeds the air,
but it takes bacteria until well
after dinner to begin to form
complex multicellular beings.

Thus begins the Cambrian explosion,
when evolution transcends itself.
If you have gumption for a climb
in the Canadian Rockies the results
can be seen on the Burgess Shale,
a vast cliff face packed with fossils.

For many millions of years
these rocks are buried in silt
at the bottom of the ocean
before a massive tectonic shift
lifts them two thousand feet
to shape the side of a mountain.

Then for eons glaciers slowly
scrape these gray slabs into view.
If you ask what has five eyes
and a nose like a vacuum cleaner,
or eight legs and as many spines,
the answer can be seen here.

Although they thrive for three-
hundred million years, as continents
drift apart, oceans and temperatures
rise and fall, crucial adaptions
of eyes and a backbone, most
of these creatures are extinct.

Global warming does them in.
Catastrophic volcanic eruptions
heat up the planet to the point
where all the trilobites die
and so do ninety percent
of other living things.

In earth's grand scheme condensed
to a day it is around midnight
when we homo sapiens arrive.
For some five-and-a-half billion years
we aren't even on the scene.
Now, chances are, the party's over.

Scientists tell us the planet
is near a point of no return,
a combination of climate change
and loss of habitat means precious
species and ecosystems are dying
off faster than we can study them.

The culprit is fossil fuels.
We use gas and oil from
the compressed carbon
of plants and other organisms
that lived eons before us,
making our planet unfit for life.

Is there hope: yes and no:
informed people already know
what needs to be done:
switch to renewable energy,
change our wasteful habits.
Will we do what is necessary?

Probably not, not in time.
Our country has done its best
to pollute the planet while
too many deny the crisis exists,
and most people won't give up
their comforting addictions.

We've known for decades
global warming is a lethal threat
but we refuse to listen
and we refuse to act—
midnight is nigh, my friends,
and fossil time is here.

About the Author

William Heath was born in Youngstown, Ohio, on June 27th, 1942. He attended Hiram College and received his M.A. and Ph.D. in American Studies from Case Western Reserve. He has taught American literature and creative writing at Kenyon, Transylvania, Vassar, and the University of Seville, serving as the Fulbright professor of American literature for two years. In 1981 he began teaching at Mount Saint Mary's University, where he edited *The Monocacy Valley Review*, which won national awards for excellence. In 2007 he retired as a Professor Emeritus. The William Heath Award is given annually to honor a student writer. In 2008-9 he was the Sophia M. Libman Professor of Humanities at Hood College.

Heath's novel about the civil rights movement in Mississippi, *The Children Bob Moses Led* (Milkweed Editions 1995, paperback 1997), won the Hackney Literary Award for best novel, was nominated for the National Book Award and the Pulitzer Prize, and by Joyce Carol Oates for the Ainsfield-Wolf Award. *Time* magazine judged it one of eleven outstanding novels on the African-American experience www.time.com/time/2002/bhm/reading.html. A twentieth anniversary edition was published by NewSouth Books in 2014. His second novel, *Blacksnake's Path: The True Adventures of William Wells* (Heritage Books 2008), was nominated for the James Fenimore Cooper Award and chosen by the History Book Club as an alternate selection. *Devil Dancer* (Somondoco Press 2013) is a neo-noir crime novel set in Lexington, KY. *William Wells and the Struggle for the Old Northwest* (University of Oklahoma Press 2015, paperback 2017) won two Spur Awards for best history book and best first nonfiction book. He also edited *Conversations with Robert Stone* (University of Mississippi Press 2016, paperback 2018). He has published numerous book reviews and twenty essays on literature and history.

Heath began publishing his poetry in the late sixties; the finest poems are collected in *The Walking Man* (Icarus Books 1994). James Wright said of this early work: "William Heath is in my opinion one of the most brilliantly accomplished and gifted young poets to appear in the United States in quite some time. I am especially moved by the delicacy and precision of the language, which indicates a distinguished intelligence, and by the purity and depth of feeling in all of his poems." Richard Wilbur noted: *"The Walking Man* is the work of a poet who knows how to tell a story."

Recently he has returned to his first love. *Steel Valley Elegy* (Kelsay Books 2022), contains a selection of his later work set in the U.S. and includes poems from a chapbook, *Night Moves in Ohio* (Finishing Line Press 2019). Kit Hathaway noted that these poems "are by turns poignant, funny, and starkly realistic . . . teeming with fascinating storyline detail and imagery," Eamon Grennan added, "These poems are savvy and lively, as exact as a high jumper's focus, quick and accurate as a tennis player's eye, wrist, ankle. . . . Heath's own remembrance of things past—an autobiography in rapt miniature lit by the laser-light of memory."

Going Places, set abroad, is the companion volume to *Steel Valley Elegy.* The first section is inspired by two years in Seville; the second draws on stays in Barcelona, home of his wife Roser. The third features their travels in Europe, while the final section tours the world, including places only visited vicariously. The extensive collection ranges from sophisticated European pleasures to the misery endured by people in remote countries. All the poems display an eye for telling detail, a lucid perspective, a sensibility that is ironic, witty, thoughtful, and compassionate, a love of sonorous words and memorable narrative, a knack for the poetic line, and a deft way of moving each poem down the page. *Going Places* is the mature work of a singular poet.

He and his wife, Roser Caminals-Heath—Professor Emerita of Spanish at Hood College and author of ten novels in Catalan—lived in Frederick, MD, since 1981 and moved to Annapolis in 2022.

Visit: williamheathbooks.com